For You

© 2009 Oliver Luke Delorie

Published by Creative Culture

Library and Archives Canada
Cataloguing in Publication

Delorie, Oliver, 1975-
Money magic : 8 powerful keys to unlock your
potential & open doors to unlimited abundance /
Austin Partridge.

ISBN 978-0-9735918-2-8

1. Finance, Personal. 2. Self-actualization
(Psychology). I. Title.

HG179.D4405 2009   332.024
C2009-901717-2

Money Magic was written for educational purposes.
This is not the first book of recycled clichés,
nor the last. Credit to all those before me.

First Edition Printed June 2009

My mission is to publish educational
and inspirational multimedia resources
to empower creatives of all ages.

Money Magic

8 Powerful Keys
To Unlock Your Potential &
Open Doors To Unlimited Abundance

PUBLISHING
A Division Of
Creative Culture

Say
Thank
You

The 4 Keys To Money

The 4 Keys To Magic

The 4 Keys To Money

*Trust
Yourself*

The 4 Keys To Money

In this book I present eight powerful keys to unlock your potential and open doors to unlimited abundance.

No matter what economic conditions you find yourself scared of, if you have the patience, time and motivation to pursue your goals, you can do whatever you want, no matter who says otherwise. Who do you listen to?

The first 4 Money Keys are all about the practical side of money, how it flows into and out of your life, and how you can become a master plumber, opening or closing the tap at will, morning, noon and night.

The ideas in this book are based on sound financial practices, personal development wisdom and playful provocation. All you need to do is take responsibility for how your thoughts - and therefore your actions - create your life and everything in it.

Every man-made object began as an idea in someone's head. You have roughly 60,000 of the same thoughts everyday. What are you thinking about?

Read this book three (3) times, think about it, talk about it, and watch what happens. You will see the world with new eyes, and it will be absolutely electrifying!

*The More
You Learn*

*

*The More
You Earn*

The Key To Earning

*You Get
What You
Give*

1. Create Value

If you want to earn money, people must find value in what you do. Create value and you will be hiring help before you know what happened. People want products and services that enhance their lives. Build it, guerilla market it - if you have way more time than money - and they will come. The cream rises to the top. No way it cannot. The greater the value, the greater the rewards. People pay handsomely for lasting value, just like you do. They always have and they always will.

2. Quality

When you find a gap that needs filling, are offering a valuable product or service, deliver the goods - tangible or intellectual - in such high quality, you and your offerings are absolutely irresistible to your customers and clients. They will praise you to their countless friends, associates and family members. Hone your skills, produce quality widgets or tangible ideas, and refine your methods to serve the public in the best way you see fit. Whatever you choose to put your heart and soul into, if you want a taste of unlimited abundance, put every effort into improving the quality of your intellectual or physical property, and you will be overwhelmed with calls, orders, deliveries and praise. How will that feel? Quantity will rarely equal quality.

Your Thoughts Are Things

3. Work For Free

One of the best ways to learn a new skill, meet the movers and shakers, and further your personal and professional goals, is to volunteer or intern at a company - or with a mentor - who can show you the ropes and give you a push in the right direction. You will grow faster by being around people doing what you want to do. Can anyone say night job? If it was easy, success would not be any fun, and would leave you wanting more. The more challenges you face, the more you will enjoy the rewards of your energy, focus and personal power. Work for free and you will see.

4. Learn To Earn

Go back to school, take a night course, sign up for correspondence, go to the library, buy some used books, watch public television and listen to public radio. Find a mentor who does what you want to do. Ask questions and listen. Soak up all you can. Follow the bread crumbs and the clues will be revealed, always whetting your appetite for more. Spend every available minute of free time either reading about your business, industry or area of expertise, or practice your sport, write your book, or get together with a group of like-minded people and brainstorm for everyone. Cooperating with others to achieve your personal and professional goals will create more than enough opportunities to go around.

Get Out Of
Your Own Way

5. Model A Winner

Be a copy-cat. Do something quicker, better, faster, smoother, cleaner, bigger, smaller, longer, taller, more efficient, cheaper, flashier, more colourful, brighter, lighter, darker, sturdier, more moveable, or whatever. You do not have to reinvent the wheel; just make it better. Modeling a winner saves you time, money and energy. Look around you and improve something to increase the quality of life. When you have an idea, find someone who had it already and learn from their mistakes and successes. Write a business plan and ask other people for their input. Start associating with professionals. Do you want boredom or excitement?

6. You Gotta Want It

No matter what you do, do it with joy and reckless abandon. What else is life for? You have to want what you want. Bad enough to stop at nothing to get it. You have to enjoy the game, otherwise why are you playing? Why are you doing what you do? If you do not find an answer, you had better stop and ask again. Do not wait for others to make you rich, famous, talented, connected, happy or in the right place at the right time. Say to yourself that if it is meant to be, it is up to me! When you are following your mission - decided only by you - you will find resources jumping into your lap, almost out of the blue.

You Can

7. Your Own Business

One sure way to financial independence is owning and enjoying your own business. Mind your own business is great advice. Decide to do more of what you love to do, get good - or better - at it, charge fair prices and take your product, service or creative project to market. Your life will never be the same again. Study other businesses that interest you. Talk to the owners and ask them what they like about running their businesses and what they could do without. See yourself working with other people towards a common goal. Perhaps you can partner with others whose skill sets compliment yours. The natural abilities you were born with are valuable. You can do anything you set your mind to. Start today.

8. Partnering

If you do not have what you need, find someone who does, and work together toward a common goal. They will benefit and so will you. Everyone wins. Nothing great has ever been accomplished alone. Figure out what you do best, then figure out what you are not so keen on. Identify what you need, then go out and find someone to fill in the blanks. Two heads are better than one, and there are people out there with similar goals and dreams, who are looking for people just like you. Find them, work together, have fun, earn some money and share it. Life can be fun.

Give Your Best
For Thirty Days
And See What
Happens

The Key To Saving

There's Enough To Go Around

1. Compound Interest

Continually make your withdrawals less than your deposits, and Einstein's Eighth Wonder Of The World will take over, making you richer every day. Just put more money into your savings account than you take out, or take out less than you put in. Of course, you need to spend less money than you make, but you already know that. Keep shopping for the highest interest rate you can get; the energy you put out will literally pay off. Find a compounding interest table on the internet and you will be amazed at how regular, untouched deposits will grow into a bundle for you to enjoy when you retire sooner than later. Just reinvest your interest and dividends.

2. Conserve Your Energy

It takes more time, energy and resources to earn a dollar than it does to save it. Every time you want to buy something, stop and think about what you will get. Will you be happier? This is why you spend money in the first place, no? Take stock of your material possessions. Do they keep you company? Some keep you warm at night, but most likely, you are still paying for them, with interest on top. With more free time, physical energy and a fatter savings account, you will have more freedom than you thought possible. The best things in life are not things, but you knew that too, right?

Save At Least
10% Of What
You Earn

3. Keep It Simple

You've heard KISS many times. Keep It Simple Stupid. Keep It Simple Sweetheart. However you like to be kissed, remember the wisest people of all time have known the freedom in simple living. Possessions will never make you happy and hopefully you know you cannot buy love. Reduce the amount of money you spend on things you do not need. Have monthly yard sales. Go camping in your own backyard. Drink more water and grow your own food. Look after your own kids or learn how to fix your own car. Buy a neighbourhood law mower. Why is everything so complicated? Simplify your life and celebrate it.

4. True Wealth

Real wealth is free time. You can always earn more money. Your time is at a premium; the most valuable commodity in your portfolio, so covet yours like it is all you have. When you are in control of your own schedule, you will be able to relax more, try new things, do whatever you like, whenever you want. Maybe you would like to toss your alarm clock and sleep in. Sure you will not be wasting your money doing the things everyone else does to distract themselves. You may have to find new friends, because all of your old friends are stuck in jobs they hate, miserable, tired, unhappy and unproductive.

*Imagine
Everyone Is
Enlightened
Except You*

5. Freedom Is Fun

Freedom is stress-busting. Are you stressed out? Get out of debt, job share, reduce your expenses and/or freelance your skills to your employer. You may think owning things gives you more freedom; you can go quadding, boating, fishing, racing, or whatever, but as long as you are paying for stuff or experience, you will not be free. You may be scared if you have always thought more stuff would make you happy. Joyful things in life like love, friends and laughing are free, and will always be. Save your money and keep it saved. Use it to buy time instead of stuff you do not need to please people you do not like.

6. Sleep On It

Before you go out and buy a new car, new suit, evening gown, new house or new big toy, sleep on it. You may be stuck with payments you cannot afford. If you are wise, you will have saved up for whatever want you are wanting. An even better strategy is to (only) spend the interest your investments make. This is what rich people do. Be patient and save your money. Do you want to be working for the rest of your life? Hopefully you want to sleep in once in a while, have a leisurely breakfast with your spouse, kids or pet, meet friends for lunch and not have to rush back to work. You want to enjoy your life, right? You have enough shoes.

*Reality Is
In The Eyes
Of The Beholder*

7. The Best Things In Life Are Free

The smartest, happiest and most successful people in the world care little about money. They know what is important. Do you? If you are in debt, you are trapped. Do you want to be trapped? Are you getting tired of going in circles and not getting anywhere? The way out is to save ten percent of every cent you make - no matter what - and do things that make you feel great.

8. Money To Invest

The more money you save, the more money you have to invest in your own business, in holidays, in free time, or in learning a new skill or trade. You will have so much fun with your new-found wealth - that was always there - you will not want to (or have to) work more than you feel it, ever again. You will have the resources to invest in any number of life-enhancing pursuits. Surely you can come up with a few ideas on how to invest your money. You can invest in paints, dance or voice lessons, fresh food to cook and bake with, days of sunshine to warm and nourish your body, a dock at the lake, or a boat to go fishing. Do what you love. Travel the world if you want. Go get the best education on earth. Make your money work for you, instead of the other way around. Do you like being a slave when you do not have to be?

The Best Things
In Your Life
Are Free

The Key To Spending

*Earn More
Than You Spend*

*

*Or Spend Less
Than You Earn*

1. Buy Appreciating Assets

Spend your money on assets that appreciate in value. When you buy something new, the minute you take it home it is worth less than what you paid for it. This is called depreciation. Learn the difference between assets and liabilities and you will be steps ahead. In business, the rule is: you earn money when you buy, not when you sell. Invest in quality and then spend the money these investments make, instead of spending the money you make. As long as they earn more money than they cost, you will be on your way to mastering your financial life, inside and out.

2. Mind Your Own Business

Spend money on your own business and you will see great returns. If only for the peace of mind you get having your money close to home, investing in yourself is wise. If you want to succeed, invest in your business. Perhaps buying a new computer or office equipment will add to the productivity of your business empire. Maybe you need a truck. Maybe some art supplies. Remember the 80-20 rule. Eighty percent of the output (sales) come from twenty percent of the input (products/services). Twenty percent of results come from eighty percent of the output, so focus only on what produces the greatest results in your business, and in your life. This is powerful and highly effective. Try it.

Act Like You Can't Lose

3. Enjoy It

Life is meant to be enjoyed. One of the best ways to take control of your time and financial life is to offer the products or services - you alone - seem especially equipped to provide. If you do not enjoy what you do, you will be miserable. No matter how much money you earn, no matter how much power you accumulate, no matter how famous you become, if you are not happy, there is no point. If you have forgotten your anniversary or missed the Christmas concert at junior's elementary school, you are missing out. If you are not happy with how things are going, have the courage to change. It may not be comfortable, but it will be a lot more comfortable than not changing, and being miserable for the rest of your life. What fun is that going to be?

4. Educate Yourself

No matter what your goals are - personal or professional - there have been countless others who have gone before you, and profited enormously doing what you dream of doing. Spending money on an education is one of the most valuable investments you will ever make, whether night classes, books, seminars, or a degree. Student loan or new car? The car will depreciate. Your mind (hopefully) will not. You will pay for both, but with some smarts, you will have more money to make the payments. The more you learn, the more you earn.

*If You
Believe It*

*

*You'll
Achieve It*

5. Negotiating

Everything in life is negotiable. Prices are arbitrary and haggling will not only amuse you, but also get you the best deals, especially if you learn how to do it. Go to the library, borrow a book or three, and learn the tricks of the trade. How do the best negotiators do it? Go to a seminar and take notes. Search for resources on how to become a win-win negotiator. These skills will help in all areas of your life. You will get what you want more often that not. You do not get what you deserve; you get what you negotiate.

6. There Are No Rules

Just because your mother, father, pastor or teacher told you it could not be done, does not mean squat. If you want to do something, do it. Do not worry what other people think. They are too concerned with what you think about them. Sure, you want to go about your business without harming other people, but when it comes to trying something new and taking risks, ask yourself: what is life for anyway? Do you want to be 80 and look back at your life - possibly alone - and wonder why you did not laugh more, dance more, take more holidays, trust more, love more, sing more, or whatever? You will not regret the things you did. You will regret the things you did not do. Ask and you will receive. Knock and the door will be opened.

If You Want
Something
To Change

*

Change
The Way You
Look At It

7. Give It Away

If you want to have more money than you have ever had before, give it away and let it go. When you can do this without the slightest feeling of discomfort, you will have unlocked the biggest door of all, and will either be showered with so much money you are overwhelmed, or it will not matter. You will reach a state few people experience. Likely, you will enjoy both sides of the coin, and either way, you will be a lot better off. You will actually be happy every day. Can you imagine that? What would that be like? What would you do? Who would be there? Where would you be? How would it feel? Take a moment and picture what that will be like, because this and more is possible. The more you prosper others, the more others will prosper you.

8. Put $100 In Your Pocket

Go to your bank and take out a $100 bill. Put it in your pocket, purse or wallet and keep in there. It will remind how rich you are. If you ever spend it, go take out another one. When you start questioning your survival, contemplating poverty or lack of whatever it may be, take out that $100 and look at it. Even if this is the only $100 you have, feel how rich you are. Many people have turned less into more, almost overnight. Empower yourself. Learn the 8 Keys to Money Magic. You have nothing to lose, but everything to gain.

You Have
Everything
You Need

The Key To Investing

If There's A Will

*

There's A Way

1. Educate Yourself

When it comes to trusting someone else to invest your hard-earned dollars and cents, you at least want to know their track record, present and former clients, and their personal investing habits. Educate yourself about the person or company who will be playing around with your loot. If your money is important to you - which it is - spend time learning the costs involved, when you will be paid back, and with how much interest. If you get a bad feeling about anything, trust your intuition and choose another way to create money out of thin air. See negative experiences as fuel for your inner fire.

2. Get Out Of Debt

One of the best investments you can make is to get out of debt. There are few investments paying returns like you will get by paying off your credit cards - as soon as possible. Why would you want a ten percent return when you pay the credit card company eighteen? The calm you will experience will give you the clarity, time and patience to make informed decisions, eventually leading to positive changes in absolutely every area of your life. Debt is slavery. Get out of debt as soon as possible and begin investing in either your own education, your own business or an income-producing asset or three. You will be happy you did. And so will your kids. Teach them some Money Magic.

*To Avoid
Criticism:
Do Nothing
Be Nothing
Say Nothing*

3. Invest In Yourself

Invest in yourself and your natural talents and abilities. The most satisfying rewards will come from your input of time, energy, money and resources into your life. You will also know where your money is going. No one cares about your resources - financial or otherwise - like you. If you want to turn a hobby into a business, invest in inventory or software. Invest in an education. Buy a book on marketing. Effectively market a quality product or service and you will never have a sleepless night worrying about money again. Take a business professional out to lunch and soak up their wisdom and experience like a sponge. If you get jealous of someone, go and get what you want.

4. Excitement

Invest in things that excite you. What excites you? What do you love? How do you want to feel about what you have invested in? How well do you want to sleep at night? What do you find yourself saying *YES* to? If you are not excited about your investments, they will not bring you pleasure, happiness or enjoyment. You might as well be investing in anti-depressants. What else is life for? We do not stop playing because we get old. We get old because we stop playing. If anyone tries to rain on your parade, keep marching. Are you going to let someone else's imaginary fears get in your way?

There Is No Limit

5. Let Go

If you like to gamble, risk your disposable income and let go of the results. There is no point in tossing and turning all night if you are worried about your investments. Life is too short. Allocate some money for risky investments and let go of it. Otherwise play it safe and find hobbies, crafts, local businesses or creative projects to put your time, money and energy into; something that inspires you. Letting go is the secret skeleton key to Money Magic. When you get this key on your ring and know how to use it, you are unstoppable. Nothing can get to you. No more money worries. There is nothing like giving up regret about the past or fear of the future. Letting go always works.

6. Pride Of Ownership

If you are not proud of your investments, they will do you no good. Again, what is the point of dragging your self-esteem or confidence down? Investments you are enthusiastic about will pay more than dividends over the course of your personal and professional life. The same goes for your home, your car, your wardrobe. Of course, you ideally want to be proud of who you are, otherwise it is impossible to be proud of anything in your life. When it comes to people and relationships, just remember you do not own anyone, so stop trying. Invest in the people and projects that inspire you.

Ignore It
And You Will
Get More Of It

7. Invest In Your Own Backyard

One of the greatest pleasures in life is seeing the fruits of your labor, up close and personal. Waking up every day to revel in the results of your work is a true joy, and can satisfy and satiate your appetite for achievement in ways only investing in your own backyard can. Whether it is an apartment block on the corner, or an ice cream stand by the lake, you are most likely a valuable member of your community if you invest where you live. Maybe the local softball team needs a coach or a sponsor. Maybe the community center needs some renovations. Perhaps you can volunteer your services, expertise or financial assistance to build a teen center to keep kids engaged in activities that benefit everyone.

8. Future Financial Freedom

Even though focusing only on the future will leave you wondering where your life went, it makes sense to invest for a rainy day. Do you want to be working when you are 60? It is easier to save money than to make it. If you have the choice of making $100 or saving it, choose to save it. After you pay tax, you only have $85. Choose another profession, or one that provides a lifestyle you want. As long as you are happy, nothing else matters. If you can learn to live simply, dancing the hokey-pokey is what it is all about, in case you have ever wondered why life seems so silly sometimes.

Breathe Before
You Speak

Money Magic Memories

_____

_____

_____

_____

_____

_____

_____

_____

_____

_____

_____

_____

_____

_____

The 4 Keys To Magic

Being Right Makes Everyone Else Wrong

The 4 Keys To Magic

The second part of Money Magic is more magical than practical. However you like to think of the god force powering everything from ant hills to nuclear power plants, the 4 Keys to Magic are about what you cannot see, and are therefore more important than money.

You are in the right place at the right time. The only thing you need to do differently than what you do now, is recognize how your thoughts and feelings are attracting people and experiences into your life. Trust that you can attract or repel anything you want.

When you see the trickle of abundance flowing into your life, you will be amazed at how a simple shift in thinking was all it took, and you will ask yourself why you had not seen the world this way years before.

It is never too late to try new things, take risks, and live the life you dream about. You will make new friends, earn more money, do the things you have always wanted, and wonder why everyone seems like they are sleepwalking their way through life.

Learn to appreciate the limitless abundance surrounding you. Doors will open in a blink of an eye, and you will be showered with more gifts and joy than you can possibly share. Just imagine!

*Your Altitude
Is Equal To
Your Attitude*

The Key To Thinking

*Keep Asking
Yourself*

*

*What Is
Important?*

1. Think For Yourself

One of the most important ways to change your life, your relationships and your bank balance, is to stop thinking so much about what other people think about you and what you do, and start thinking new thoughts, regardless of other people's opinions. If you want to be free, trust your own sense of justice and take the action necessary to achieve your goals. No one is going to do it for you. No one will ever care about you or your plans like you do. Think of ways to get what you want and muster the courage to do whatever it takes. You are your choices. Start thinking for yourself.

2. Get Creative

When you know how your thoughts create your life, you will not need to do as much, but you will get more done. You are immeasurably creative and full of ability. All you need to do is trust this enough to take a risk. The only time you fail is if you give up before you reach your goal. All you have to do is persevere. You are your only enemy. If you really want something, brainstorm for an hour or two how to get it, or get a group of friends together for feedback and encouragement. There are as many ways to live as there are people on the planet. If there is a will, there is a way. There is no limit to what you can do. Everything you see began with a simple thought, so start thinking outside of the box.

Are You
Motivated By
Fear Or By Love?

3. Mirrors

One of the best ways to find out what you believe is to take a look at your life. What is working? What is not? Your life - absolutely everything in it - is a result of the thoughts you have been thinking since the day you were born. Sure, your parents, siblings, teachers, the television and other authority figures had some influence in how you turned out, but are they to blame? Take responsibility for your actions and watch how much abundance you attract. Take a single step toward your goals each and every day, based on how you feel. Scared? Do it anyway. You will be amazed at how good you feel. Look at your reflection in the mirror of your life. What do you see? If something bugs you, that is because it bugs you when you do it too.

4. Ask New Questions

If you want to see magic in your effortless efforts to change the conditions in your financial, love, social and home lives, you will need to ask new questions if you want new answers. If you keep doing the same things over and over again, you are going to keep getting the same results, over and over again. Now if you keep doing the same things over and over and are expecting different results, then you need to take a good look in the mirror and ask yourself who you think you are fooling. Expect answers and opportunities.

Life Is But
A Dream

5. Go For A Walk

Turn off your TV, go for a walk and take some deep breaths. This will clear your head and get you thinking differently. Not only good for your body, exercise gets you naturally high and keeps you healthy. Without great health, no amount of money, abundance or prosperity will matter. Health is your greatest wealth. Slowing down and taking it easy will generate good thoughts. You will be happier when you are active and your mind is not spinning out of control. Anything that relaxes you will produce not only exceptional health, but some great ideas, and the inspiration to make them a reality.

6. You Are Your Choices

The wisest people have always known we become what we think about, just like we are what we eat (we have all heard that one). Your beliefs have always decided the paths you have taken, and will continue to do so until you realize how these unconscious conclusions are motivating you. Decide to believe in magic instead of mud and make deliberate choices, so you get more of what you want and less of what you do not. Your life is a result of your choices. When you find yourself about to put something on plastic when you would like to save money, you have a choice. This is the first day of the rest of your life. Choose how you want it to be from now on, even one small baby step at a time.

The Bitter
Makes The Sweet
Even Better

7. Focus

When you want to manifest the conditions necessary to realize your deepest desires, wishes, wants and dreams, you have to focus. If you can think, you can focus. If you can drive, talk, cook, walk or read, you have the ability to focus. This is essential to creating magic in your life. All you need to do is focus on something long enough to create a lasting impression. See it like it is real. Like you are already doing it, being it, or having what you want. It is easy. You just have to get out of the way, and keep your other thoughts - the ones that say "no way" - from interfering in your private fantasy. If you can focus with enough intent and imagination, there is no end to what you can create.

8. Courage

It takes courage to be different and to try new things, especially when it seems like everyone around you is scared of change, or on autopilot all day long. The truth is, if you really want to create miracles in your life, you have to step out of line every once in a while and stop following the herd like a sheep. You need courage to try new things, because that is the only way you will get what you want. Try facing a fear. Chances are, whatever you were scared of was not as frightening as you thought it would be. Remember what it was like when you realized you did not have to be afraid.

*Turn Lead
Into Gold*

The Key To Feeling

You Get What You Expect

1. Write It Down

We think in words, see words, talk in words and write words, all day long. Words are powerful. Do you ever listen to the words you say to yourself, or to other people? What words do you use when you talk to your spouse, partner, kids or parents? If you want to create something out of nothing, it helps to see it on paper. Using words to describe your goals, intentions and visions can create clarity and help you manifest them sooner. Keep a journal or draw pictures of your daily thoughts and feelings. Watch for connections between how you feel, and what is happening in your life. This is an incredibly powerful way to get the magic flowing.

2. Take A Test Drive

On your next day off, go down to the nearest car dealership selling the car you want to own and take it for a test drive. It does not matter if you have the money yet, just go and drive it. Have fun. Feel the leather, feel the air on your face with the top down, smell the new car smell. Lick the dashboard when no one is looking! Soak it up and take it all in. Next, go to an open house for sale in the area of town you would like to live. See yourself living in that house. Lease the car and rent the house. Maintain perspective, so when the things you own eventually own you, you can let go of them at a moment's notice if you have to.

Do You Want Peace?

*

Forgive Your Enemies

3. You Deserve It

You deserve to be happy and to feel good. You were born without fears, worries, hopes or dreams. You had a clean slate and an open mind. You can do what you want. No one is stopping you. If you think someone or something is standing in your way, take a good look at yourself and ask who or what is really in your way. The answer may surprise you. If you want something bad enough, you will find a way to get it. Follow your heart instead of your head and you will get everything you desire. Start living how you have always imagined, and you will meet with a success even sweeter than you could ever have dreamed up on your own.

4. Make It Into A Movie

Close your eyes and picture a time in your life you were scared or angry or embarrassed or ashamed, and take a step outside of the picture. Clone yourself - create another you in the picture - and notice how you actually detach from what is happening. No more negative effects. Add some circus music to make it seem silly, if that helps you laugh about it. If fears of any kind are keeping you from going out and getting what you want, stop dwelling on them. You survived. You made it, and it is time to start living. It is time to be the person you want to be. The only thing stopping you is fear. False Evidence Appearing Real. That is all.

A Friend Is Worth More Than Gold

5. Breathe

Set aside 10 minutes every day and take one deep breath after another. You will relax so much you will see the world in a different light. Do this enough, and you will free yourself from attachment to past histories and future mysteries. You will tune your personal radio to the frequencies of love, money, happiness, health and joy, simply by seeing it, tasting it, touching it, hearing it and/or pretending you already enjoy it. It all starts in your imagination, so calm yourself down. This is all you need to do. Take a deep breath. Now do it again.

6. Visualize

When you visualize, you materialize. Imagination is more important than knowledge, said Einstein. Explore the unexplored, right where you sit. Creative visualization is such an easy way to create magic in your life. Find some books or CDs and devote a little time every day to creating some miracles in your life. When you combine the pictures, sounds, feelings, tastes and smells in your head, nothing is beyond your grasp. Just keep focusing on the images and/or feelings of your personal sense of success and abundance, and you will see the results, faster than you can say Money Magic. Just stop thinking a whole bunch of depressing thoughts at the same time, or you will keep going around in circles. That is no fun.

*If You Want To
Make God Laugh
Just Tell Him
Your Plans*

7. Make It Happen

If you want something bad enough, do whatever you have to do. If you have doubts, ignore them. You have to pretend they matter not. Do you want to let some imaginary stage fright get in your way? How important is your life? How do you want to feel everyday? Get out there and do what you want to do. Just do it. If you need money, find it. If you need support, find it. If you need materials, find them. If you need a kick in the pants, get a friend or coach to motivate you. Imagine what your ideal day looks like, then do everything in your power to make it happen. Follow your heart. You know how.

8. Let Your Emotions Guide You

Your feelings are the best guide you have. If you are doing something and want to know if it is in your best interest, just ask God, Buddha, your inner child, higher self, the universe, power animal - or whoever you revere - just how you feel. If you feel good, keep doing what feels good. Listen to what your feelings say. Every feeling and impression you have is either constructive or destructive. What do you want to create? What do you want to destroy? Just pay attention. Things in life either feel good or feel bad. How do you feel right now? What are you focusing on? Is it possible or impossible? Only you can decide, but either way you are right.

Stop Thinking About What You Fear

*

Replace These Thoughts With Your Goal

The Key To Living

*You Can Always
Get More Money*

*

*You Can't Get
More Time*

1. Act It Out

Compensating for stinkin' thinkin' is no fun. Start from the beginning. Define abundance for yourself. Make it easy. Make it fun. You will be amazed at how easy it is to make your dreams come true. You are the pilot of your own plane. Whose life is it anyway? You are the only one you have to answer to, when everything is said and done. If this is not presently the case, make it so. You are in control of your life. Act like the person you want to be. Do it now. Do it tomorrow and the next day. The more you see it, the more you will do it. And the more you do it, the more you will see it. Objects at rest tend to stay at rest, and objects in motion tend to stay in motion.

2. Talk About It

Talk about your desires. Talk about being in love and about earning money, just keep the trade secrets secret. Share your dreams with others to see how it feels. Listen to how you describe it. What happens to your body when you tell others about your goals and dreams? How do you react to their feedback and/or body language? What do you think they think? If you feel uneasy or do not really believe it, you need to climb out of your cozy rut and start living. You generate good things with good thoughts, even if they do not seem possible at first. Everything is made of stuff we cannot see. See?

Actions Speak
LOUDER
Than Words

3. Be Accountable

Accountability to others - like to yourself - is an integral part of living up to your awesome potential. Go about your business without harming anyone or anything, and maintain honesty and integrity in all your personal and professional dealings. You will come out ahead and sleep soundly at night, when all is said and done. You will also have more friends than foes, which will make for smooth sailing. Do not spend too much time dwelling on the destructive elements in your life, just be aware they exist. Take responsibility for your life and remember that what you deny will betray you.

4. Group Therapy

Working with others is gratifying in ways working alone will never be. Nothing of any great significance or lasting importance has ever been - or will ever be - accomplished by flying solo. Two heads are better than one, and happiness was born a twin. Joy is a shared emotion, born when people celebrate life together. Meet once a week with like-minded friends, business associates, a networking group, your family, employees or an imaginary group of living - or dead - personal heros (talk about a free consultation). If you only knew who walked beside you. You have never been alone, nor will you ever be. The more we get together, the happier we will be, because friends are worth more than gold.

*If You Want To
Be In Show
Business
Get Out Of
The Factory*

5. Fake It Til You Make It

Sounds funny, but it works. Practice whatever you want to be in the future - now. When you give yourself permission to live the life you have always imagined, it actually happens. You have your finger on the pulse, creating your life how you wish. Dress for success. Take care of yourself. Give yourself the best of everything, even if it is scary. The scarier it is, the more important it is. You have nothing to lose. What is the worst that can happen? When you are dead, nothing will matter. If you are going to heaven, your sins are forgiven anyway, so you got nothing to lose. Even if it is raining cats and dogs, get out of bed and pretend your life is great.

6. The Proof Is In The Pudding

Take note of your successes; past, present, big and small. If you attract information, a book, a cup of coffee, a compliment or a prize, congratulate yourself! Believe - without a doubt in the world - you will meet your goals. Doubt is the worst enemy you have. Forget lions and tigers and bears. You are your own worst enemy, which is why you need to remind yourself why you do what you do. Celebrate with your friends when you reach your goals, however simple they may be. You know you have what it takes. You can do it. Prove it. If not to yourself, to the people closest to you. They want you to succeed; they are itching for all the perks.

*Your Past
Is History*

*

*Your Future's
A Mystery*

7. An Attitude Of Gratitude

By giving thanks for everything in your life, you allow more good things to show up. This is good. By saying "Thank You" you see doors where there were only walls. This is the nature of reality. Appreciate your eyes, your ears, your lungs, your brain, your legs, your fingers; whatever you can give thanks for. You have everything you need. This is contentment. The more you appreciate, the more opportunities you will get to appreciate even more. Now you are connected to the source from which everything originates and are ripe for all kinds of goodies to show up. Bless the things you love and you get more of the same. Guaranteed.

8. Feel The Fear & Do It Anyway

You are ready. You attracted this book; a good sign. If you trust in what you do - and why - and your passion is strong enough to melt steel, you will do what needs to be done, even with butterflies bashing around in your stomach. The more you do things that scare you, the more courage you will have to achieve bigger and better things. And not only for yourself, but for others, because sharing your wealth - in whatever form it takes - will give you a pleasure no amount of money will ever buy, no matter how good you get at Money Magic. Under no circumstances, do not let fear stop you. You were born to kick some ass doing what you love.

*Your Life
Is A Garden*

*

*You Pick What
You Plant*

The Key To Sharing

Do You Want To Get Rich?

*

You Just Have To Enrich Others

1. Givers Get

A sure way to get more of anything - if you really want it - is to give it away. As much as you can, to those who need it. When you let go of your tight-fisted, gripping attachment to things both visible and invisible, regardless of their sentimental value, you will finally know what life is all about. Relinquishing your need to accumulate material things will either make you so blissful and happy, you either need nothing else to satisfy your hunger and thirst for more, or you will have everything in so much abundance, you will find immeasurable pleasure sharing your wealth with all who cross your path. Social or economic status, age, height, religious beliefs, sex, race or ideology of the recipient of your gifts will cease to matter. It is only with the heart that one can see rightly. What is most important is invisible to the eye, says the Little Prince.

2. Listen

We are connected to everyone and everything in the multiverse when we really listen to someone. Surprisingly, this is all some people want. Everyone is healed when we stop focusing on ourselves. One of the greatest gifts you can give is to just listen. Instead of waiting for your turn to share your opinion or give advice, just be quiet and forget about yourself for a minute. What happens?

*You Have Two Ears
And One Mouth*

*

*Listen Twice As
Much As You Talk*

3. Volunteer

Another great way to connect to your unending inner electricity is to volunteer your time, resources and/or services to a person who may benefit from your gifts. When you stop thinking about yourself and ask how you can be of service, you will find your reservoir overflowing with resources, where you thought there were none. Making friends, learning new things, eating different food, going to new places and realizing not everyone makes the same choices will change your life forever. Give in to your innate sense of curiosity. Start asking "What can I give, instead of what can I get?"

4. Teach Others

Give someone a fish, and they eat for a day. Teach someone to fish and they will eat everyday. You have skills and abilities that would benefit others, so why not teach a class or find a protegé to mentor in your line of work? Someone who reminds you of yourself; someone with the drive, passion and determination you have. People want guidance. Young people need positive role models. You remember what it was like trying to figure it all out on your own. Just think how an hour a week coaching a young person would benefit them. There is no satisfaction greater than sharing your gifts, no matter what they are. Time is your greatest asset. If you have a lot on your hands, give it away.

You Are
Your
Choices

5. Nothing Matters

Ultimately, nothing matters. We are here, then we are gone. So is everyone else, and most everything else. There is no telling what is going to happen tomorrow, though psychics think they do a pretty good job. At the end of the day, we all have struggles to face, obstacles to overcome and must learn to find meaning in our lives. Many find it easier to follow the path laid by their ancestors. For others who wish to blaze new roads, it can be difficult, but following the horse in front of us - when we want to be trailblazing - is even more disastrous, leaving us miserable and hopeless. The answer is simple. Pay attention to what makes you feel good. Share your love with everyone you meet and giggle every day. It heals all wounds and feels great.

6. Keep It Flowing

Sell or give away things you do not use anymore or have not used in a while. Someone will find great pleasure in these gifts, you can be sure, and you will have made room for more. Clutter - mental and material - blocks new stuff from showing up. The ocean of abundance is unlimited, and so are you. One of the best ways to experience bliss is to keep the energy of love, peace and material abundance flowing. Do your best to share it, give it away or let it go in whatever ways it wants. We are just cups, happiest when we are overflowing.

*Money Will Not
Bring Happiness*

*

*But Happiness
Will Bring Money*

7. There's More To Life

We do what is most important to us. If it is important, we make time. If you want to do something, you do it. Instead of focusing on what is missing in your life, notice what is working, and enjoy that. There is more to life than money. Become an alchemist and turn lead into gold. Play with your kids, or do something you have always wanted to do. Face your fears. All of them. You will live longer, smile more, and food will taste better than it ever has before. When you are totally involved in what you are doing, all the money you could ever use will make its way to you like magic. And you probably will not even notice, you are having so much fun.

8. Be Anonymous

Do you really want to be rich and famous? Do you really not value your privacy? Do you really want to have to worry about storing, insuring and protecting your stuff? Stress is the opposite of what we imagine life in the financial fast lane to be like, all glitz and glamour. Ideally, you will be happier and enjoy life more if you are not the center of attention and the envy of those who really just want to be acknowledged, listened to and respected. Let go of the need to find meaning in stuff, which is a false reflection of who you really are. Your imaginary idea of yourself is robbing you of what you really want. Surrender and allow your life to flow.

*Every Journey
Begins With
One Step*

Dear Reader,

I was once homeless, unemployed, deeply in debt, eating out of trash cans, separated from my life partner, miles from my friends and family, struggling with addiction, and drowning in the most negative of thoughts.

I read hundreds of books, listened to a thousand tapes, went to seminar after seminar and nothing seemed to be working, so I thought about what I did best.

I write songs and knew the effects they had on me, so I began writing song lyrics that inspired me.

Write your own 3 line song, hum it to a tune and a rhythm, and sing it to yourself whenever you drive, walk, load the dishwasher, fall asleep, wake up, cook dinner, rake leaves, do laundry or whatever.

I have written thousands of lyrics over the past 24 years and can help you create your own Magic Song, if you like. It is truly the simplest and most enjoyable way to reset your financial thermostat, that was set for you before you even knew who you were.

Singing your Magic Song (or whatever you want to call it) will make everything else in this book work even faster, so email me and I will help you write it for free.

oliverlukedelorie@gmail.com

Do What You Love To Do

*

The Money Will Follow You

Money Magic Memories

_____

_____

_____

_____

_____

_____

_____

_____

_____

_____

_____

_____

_____

_____

www.ingramcontent.com/pod-product-compliance
Lightning Source LLC
Chambersburg PA
CBHW071057040426
42443CB00013B/3360